SPACE: FACTS + FIGURES

THE MOON

Nancy Dickmann

Published by Brown Bear Books Ltd
Unit 1/D, Leroy House
436 Essex Road
London N1 3QP

Copyright © 2019 Brown Bear Books Ltd

ISBN 978 1 78121 488 6

For Brown Bear Books Ltd:
Text and Editor: Nancy Dickmann
Children's Publisher: Anne O'Daly
Editorial Director: Lindsey Lowe
Design Manager: Keith Davis
Designer and Illustrator: Supriya Sahai
Picture Manager: Sophie Mortimer

Concept development: Square and Circus/Brown Bear Books Ltd

Picture Credits:
Front cover: Supriya Sahai
Interior: NASA: 19, 20, 29, Apollo 16 crew 6, John Caldwell (York University, Ontario), Alex Storrs
(STScI)/ESA 22, JPL 21, JPL/USGS 17, JSC 12–13; Shutterstock: amlet 11, Astrostar 23, Baranov E 4,
Castleski 16, 25, Claudio Divizia 15, 28, Sanit Fuangnakhon 5, Irina Mos 18, Nevada31 9, Ozef 14, Tom
Reichner 8, Vadim Sadovski 27, Romolo Tavani 7, Tristan3D 26; Wikipedia: NASA 24.

Key: t=top, b=bottom, c=centre, l=left, r=right

Brown Bear Books has made every attempt to contact the copyright holder.
If anyone has any information please contact licensing@brownbearbooks.co.uk

Websites
The website addresses in this book were valid at the time of going to press. However, it
is possible that contents or addresses may change following publication of this book. No
responsibility for any such changes can be accepted by the author or the publisher. Readers
should be supervised when they access the internet.

A catalogue record for this book is available from the British Library

Printed in China

CONTENTS

WHAT IS A MOON?

Look up at the night sky. You might be able to see the moon. It is our closest neighbour in space.

The moon is special to us, but it is not unique. A moon is simply an object in space that **orbits** (travels around) another object. The 'other object' can't be a star. But it can be a **planet**, **asteroid** or **dwarf planet**. Many planets have moons.

A moon must be a natural object. A spacecraft orbiting a planet is not a moon.

People used to think that a full moon could affect people's behaviour.

The moon is sometimes bright enough to cast shadows on the ground at night.

Many religions have a god or goddess of the moon.

Some people call Earth's moon 'Luna', to distinguish it from other moons.

GO FIGURE!

Planets in the solar system: 8
Moons in the solar system that orbit planets: at least 173
Number of full moons it would take to match the sun's brightness: 398,110

TRAVELLING THROUGH SPACE

The moon is always moving. It travels in loops around Earth. At the same time, Earth is orbiting the sun.

The moon takes about 28 days to complete one **orbit** around Earth. It takes Earth a year to complete one orbit around the sun. During that time, the moon makes about 12 orbits around Earth. Its orbit isn't a perfect circle – it's slightly squashed. This means that sometimes the moon is closer to Earth than at other times.

We always see the same half of the moon. Spacecraft have taken photos of the far side.

Our word 'month' comes from the word 'moon'.

From the moon, Earth doesn't appear to move very much.

You could line up about 30 Earths to stretch from Earth to the moon.

GO FIGURE!

Average speed: 3,681 kilometres per hour
Average distance from Earth: 384,400 kilometres
Distance travelled in one orbit: 2,413,402 kilometres
Exact length of orbit: 27.322 Earth days

The moon looks so big in the sky because it is very close to us, compared to the stars and **planets**.

PHASES OF THE MOON

The moon appears to change shape as the days go by. It's all because of light and shadow.

The moon does not make its own light. It reflects light from the sun. The half of the moon that faces the sun is always bright. The other half is dark. The moon travels around Earth. At some points we can see the entire bright face. At other times, we see part of its bright side and part of its dark side.

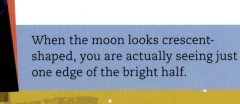

When the moon looks crescent-shaped, you are actually seeing just one edge of the bright half.

The moon's different shapes are called **phases**.

Full moon

When the moon grows bigger, we say it is waxing.

Waning gibbous

Waxing gibbous

GO FIGURE!

Full moon: full circle
Gibbous moon: more than half a circle showing
Quarter moon: half of the moon is bright
Crescent moon: less than half a circle showing
New moon: completely dark

Last quarter

First quarter

Waning crescent

Waxing crescent

When the moon grows smaller, we say it is waning.

New moon

We can't see the moon at all during a 'new moon', when the moon is between Earth and the sun.

9

ECLIPSES

On very rare occasions, the sun disappears in the middle of the day. The moon has caused a solar eclipse!

The moon and the sun appear almost exactly the same size in the sky. Every once in a while, they line up so exactly with Earth that the moon blocks out the sun for a few minutes. This is a total solar **eclipse**. Sometimes Earth passes directly between the sun and the moon. It can block the sun's light from reaching the moon. This is a lunar eclipse.

SOLAR ECLIPSE

The moon's shadow is small, so a total eclipse will only be visible from a small area of Earth's surface.

Area that sees a total eclipse

Although the sun is much bigger than the moon, it is much further away.

A solar eclipse can last several hours, but the sun will only be completely blocked for a few minutes.

If the moon doesn't cover the entire face of the sun, it is called a partial eclipse.

During a lunar eclipse, the moon can appear red.

(!) It is NEVER safe to look directly at the sun, even during an eclipse.

GO FIGURE!

Sun's diameter compared to the moon: about 403 times wider
Sun's average distance from Earth compared to the moon: about 389 times further away
Temperature drop on the moon during a lunar eclipse: 300 °C in just 90 minutes

SIZE AND MASS

The moon is much smaller than Earth. But it is still big enough to have an effect on our planet.

The more **mass** an object has, the stronger its **gravity** is. Earth's gravity keeps the moon in **orbit** around it. The moon has much less mass than Earth does, so its gravity is weaker. However, it still pulls on Earth. The moon's gravity makes the water in Earth's oceans bulge out. This is what causes high **tides** and low tides.

Gravity on the moon is weak enough for **astronauts** to bound across the surface.

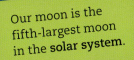

Our moon is the fifth-largest moon in the **solar system**.

The moon has about 1.2% as much mass as Earth does.

High tide

Low tide

Moon's orbit

In a 24-hour period there are two high tides and two low tides.

GO FIGURE!

Diameter of the moon:
3475 kilometres
Distance around the moon:
10,917 kilometres
Moon's gravity: 16.6% of Earth's gravity

INSIDE THE MOON

We know what the moon looks like from the outside. But what is inside the moon?

Just like Earth, the moon is divided into three layers. They sit one inside the other, like the layers of an onion. The **core** is at the centre. It is made of iron. The inner core is solid and the outer core is liquid. The **mantle** is around the core. It is made of rocky **minerals**. A thin **crust** made of hard rock is on the outside.

Olivine

The moon's mantle is made of minerals such as olivine and pyroxene. They are also found on Earth.

The moon once had **volcanoes**. They stopped erupting millions of years ago.

Inner core

Outer core

Mantle

Crust

GO FIGURE!

Inner core:
480 kilometres across
Outer core:
240 kilometres thick
Mantle:
about 1,297 kilometres thick
Crust: 70 to 150 kilometres thick, depending on the location

Earth and the moon are made of many of the same minerals.

The moon probably formed from the rocks left after a large object crashed into Earth.

ON THE SURFACE

When you look at the moon, you can see light and dark areas. They are made by different features on its surface.

The lighter areas on the moon are called highlands. The dark areas are called maria, which is Latin for 'seas'. Maria are low-lying areas that were filled with **lava** long ago, when the moon still had active **volcanoes**. Both types of land are covered with **craters**.

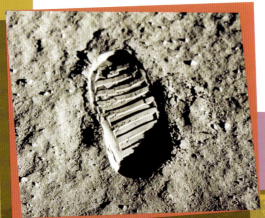

Astronauts left footprints in the powdery grey dust on the moon's surface.

The maria formed more recently than the highlands.

Mare Serenitatis (Sea of Serenity)

Copernicus crater

The top layer of the moon's surface is called the regolith.

GO FIGURE!

Oldest highland rocks: 4.51 billion years old
Age of maria: between 1.2 and 4.2 billion years old
Percentage of moon's surface covered by maria: 17%
Largest mare: Oceanus Procellarum, about 4 million square kilometres

Tycho crater

Apollo 11 landed in one of the maria, called the Sea of Tranquility.

There are hardly any maria on the far side of the moon.

CRATERS

Space rocks have been crashing into the moon for billions of years. This is how craters form.

There are many rocks in space, and they often crash into larger objects. Earth's **atmosphere** protects us from most space rocks. As the rocks travel through the gases of the atmosphere, **friction** makes them burn up. The moon does not have enough of an atmosphere to do this. Even a fairly small space rock will leave a **crater**.

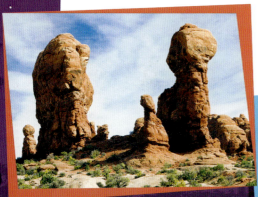

Craters and other rock formations on Earth are worn away by wind and weather. This doesn't happen on the moon.

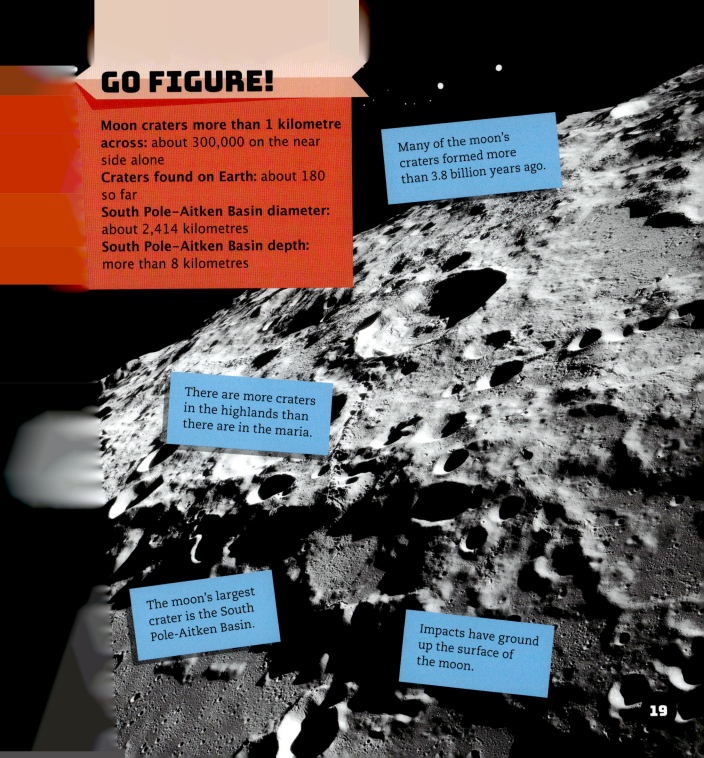

GO FIGURE!

Moon craters more than 1 kilometre across: about 300,000 on the near side alone

Craters found on Earth: about 180 so far

South Pole–Aitken Basin diameter: about 2,414 kilometres

South Pole–Aitken Basin depth: more than 8 kilometres

Many of the moon's craters formed more than 3.8 billion years ago.

There are more craters in the highlands than there are in the maria.

The moon's largest crater is the South Pole-Aitken Basin.

Impacts have ground up the surface of the moon.

HOT AND COLD

The moon is about the same distance from the sun as Earth is. Even so, it gets much hotter than Earth. And it gets much colder too.

Earth's **atmosphere** blocks some of the sun's heat during the day. It keeps heat in at night. This keeps our **temperature** fairly constant. On the moon, it is boiling hot when the sun is shining and freezing cold when it is not.

Astronauts need spacesuits with heating and cooling systems to protect them.

With no atmosphere, there is no wind, so footprints left behind by astronauts are still there.

There is ice in some deep **craters** where the sun never reaches.

Moon's north pole

The moon does not have seasons like Earth does.

Craters near the moon's south pole are some of the coldest places in the **solar system**.

GO FIGURE!

Lowest temperature: –233 °C
Highest temperature: 123 °C

LOOKING AT THE MOON

Ancient astronomers watched the moon's phases. They knew how eclipses worked. But they didn't really know what the moon was like.

In 1609, an Italian scientist called Galileo used a **telescope** to study the moon. He drew the moon's surface, showing mountains and **craters**. Other **astronomers** measured the height of its mountains and drew detailed maps. Today, we use powerful telescopes to get even closer views of the moon.

The Hubble Space Telescope can take detailed pictures of the moon's surface.

Galileo was the first person to use a telescope to study space.

Even a basic telescope can reveal many of the moon's surface features.

Many craters were mapped and named more than 350 years ago.

Astronomers hope that one day they can put telescopes on the moon.

GO FIGURE!

Galileo's telescope: magnified objects about 20 times
Tallest mountain on the moon: Mons Huygens, 5.5 kilometres high
First photos of the far side of the moon: 1959 (taken by Luna 3)
Hubble Space Telescope: 13.2 metres long, maximum diameter is 4.2 metres

VISITING THE MOON

The moon has been visited by many spacecraft. It is the only place in the solar system where astronauts have landed.

Non-crewed spacecraft first arrived at the moon in 1959. Some of them just flew past or orbited the moon. Others landed on the surface. Between 1969 and 1972, NASA sent six crewed missions to the surface of the moon. There are still several spacecraft studying the moon.

The Lunar Prospector spacecraft went into **orbit** around the moon to map its surface.

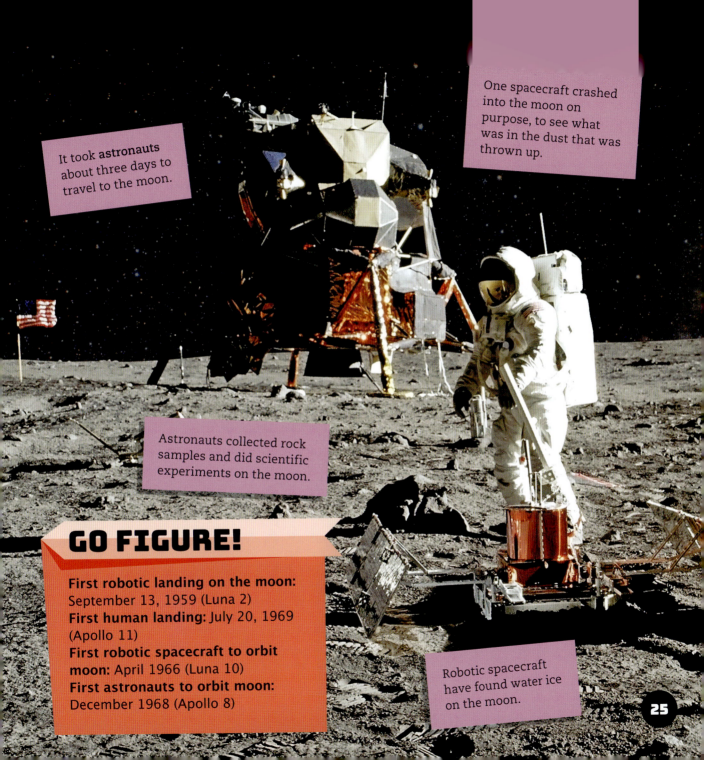

One spacecraft crashed into the moon on purpose, to see what was in the dust that was thrown up.

It took **astronauts** about three days to travel to the moon.

Astronauts collected rock samples and did scientific experiments on the moon.

GO FIGURE!

First robotic landing on the moon: September 13, 1959 (Luna 2)
First human landing: July 20, 1969 (Apollo 11)
First robotic spacecraft to orbit moon: April 1966 (Luna 10)
First astronauts to orbit moon: December 1968 (Apollo 8)

Robotic spacecraft have found water ice on the moon.

OTHER MOONS

Earth is not the only planet that has a moon. Some planets have dozens of moons!

Mars has two small moons, but the outer planets have many more. Jupiter has the most moons of any planet. Other objects, such as **asteroids** and **dwarf planets**, can have moons too. All of the moons that **astronomers** have discovered so far are rocky or icy. Some have liquid oceans beneath the surface.

Ganymede is the biggest moon in our **solar system**.

Our moon, compared in size to some of Jupiter's moons

| GANYMEDE | CALLISTO | IO | MOON | EUROPA |

Jupiter's moon Ganymede and Saturn's moon Titan are both bigger than the planet Mercury.

Some moons are asteroids that were captured by a planet's **gravity**.

Jupiter

The spacecraft Huygens landed on Titan.

Mercury and Venus are the only planets that do not have moons.

Astronomers are still finding new moons.

GO FIGURE!

Largest moon (Ganymede): 5,262 kilometres wide
Second largest moon (Titan): 5,150 kilometres wide
Earth's moon size: 5th largest of all solar system moons
Moons of Jupiter: at least 69 discovered so far

QUIZ

Try this quiz and test your knowledge of the moon! The answers are on page 32.

1 What shape is the moon's orbit around Earth?

A. a perfect circle

B. a slightly squashed circle

C. a triangle

2 What is the moon's crust made of?

A. ice

B. cheese

C. rock

3 What happens when the moon passes directly between Earth and the sun?

A. it causes a solar eclipse

B. it appears as a full moon

C. it collects £200 from the Bank

4 What holds the moon in orbit around Earth?

A. a really long rope

B. gravity

C. air pressure

5 What do we call the moon's shape when less than half of it is showing?

A. skinny

B. croissant

C. crescent

6 What are the dark patches on the moon's surface?

A. low areas filled with solid lava

B. shadows cast by Earth

C. places where the cheese has gone mouldy

7 Why are there so many craters on the moon?

A. it just hasn't found a good enough moisturizer

B. there is no atmosphere to protect the moon from space rocks

C. there is no one to sweep them away

8 What did astronauts do when they visited the moon?

A. hunted for aliens

B. collected rocks and did science experiments

C. sunbathed

GLOSSARY

asteroid a large chunk of rock left over from when the planets formed

astronaut person who travels into space

astronomer person who studies the sun, the planets and other objects in space

atmosphere a layer of gas trapped by gravity around the surface of a planet, moon or other object

core the centre of a planet, moon or some asteroids

crater circular hole made when a comet, asteroid or meteorite hits a planet or moon

crust the hard outer layer of a rocky planet, moon or some asteroids

dwarf planet object that is too small to be considered a planet, but too big to be an asteroid

eclipse when one object in space temporarily blocks out another

friction the action of one surface or object rubbing against another

gravity a force that pulls objects together. The heavier or closer an object is, the stronger its gravity, or pull.

lava melted rock that pours onto a planet's surface from underground

mantle the middle layer of some planets, moons and asteroids

mare an area of low land on the moon that has been filled in with lava

mass the measure of the amount of material in an object

mineral a solid, natural, non-living substance

orbit the path an object takes around a larger object; or, to take such a path

phase one of the different shapes the moon appears as it travels around Earth

planet large, spherical object that orbits the sun or another star

solar system a group of planets that circles a star

telescope tool used for studying space, which gathers information about things that are far away

temperature measure of how hot or cold something is

tides the regular rising and falling of sea levels due to the moon's gravity

volcanoes mountains formed from lava that erupts onto the surface from underground

FURTHER READING

Books

Astronomy, Astronauts, and Space Exploration (Watch This Space!),
Clive Gifford (Wayland Publishing, 2015)

Neil Armstrong and the Moon Landings (Why do we remember?), Izzi Howell
(Franklin Watts, 2016)

Our Solar System, Seymour Simon
(HarperCollins, 2014)

Websites

coolcosmos.ipac.caltech.edu/asks
Find a list of questions and answers about space.

nasa.gov/mission_pages/apollo/missions/index.html
Learn more about the Apollo missions that took
astronauts to the moon.

solarsystem.nasa.gov/moons/earths-moon/overview/
This NASA website has lots of information about the
moon.

INDEX

Answers to quiz:
1. b; 2. c; 3. a; 4. b; 5. c; 6. a; 7. b; 8. b